Chr... ...

To Da...

Pupa

MY SURLY HEART

Love

Dad/Tim

SOUTHERN MESSENGER POETS
Dave Smith, Series Editor

Other Books by David Huddle

POETRY

Glory River
Grayscale
Summer Lake: New and Selected Poems
The Nature of Yearning
Stopping by Home
Paper Boy
Blacksnake at the Family Reunion
Dream Sender

FICTION

Nothing Can Make Me Do This
La Tour Dreams of the Wolf Girl
Not: A Trio—A Novella and Two Stories
The Story of a Million Years
Tenorman
Intimates
The High Spirits: Stories of Men and Women
Only the Little Bone
A Dream with No Stump Roots in It
A David Huddle Reader
The Faulkes Chronicle
Hazel

ESSAYS

The Writing Habit

MY SURLY HEART

Poems

David Huddle

LOUISIANA STATE UNIVERSITY PRESS

BATON ROUGE

Published by Louisiana State University Press
Copyright © 2019 by David Huddle
All rights reserved
Manufactured in the United States of America
LSU Press Paperback Original

Designer: Michelle A. Neustrom
Typefaces: Bembo

Library of Congress Cataloging-in-Publication Data

Names: Huddle, David, 1942– author.
Title: My surly heart : poems / David Huddle.
Description: Baton Rouge : Louisiana State University Press, 2020. |
  Series: Southern messenger poets | "LSU Press Paperback Original."
Identifiers: LCCN 2019001728 | ISBN 978-0-8071-7072-4 (paper :
  alk. paper) | ISBN 978-0-8071-7233-9 (pdf) | ISBN 978-0-8071-
  7234-6 (epub)
Classification: LCC PS3558.U287 A6 2020 | DDC 811/.54—dc23
LC record available at https://lccn.loc.gov/2019001728

For my Dears, My Creatures—

Lindsey, Molly, and Bess

Ray and Nick

Hank, Hattie, and Phoebe

CONTENTS

MY SURLY HEART

Where Do You Come From?

The cosmic speck of me joined the universe
by way of my mother and my father
my brothers and my Grandmother Akers
Granddaddy and Grandmama Huddle her
kitchen his toolshop his dusty office
the help Harvey Sawyer Monkey Dunford
Thelma Lucy Uncle Will Washington Peaks
work horses cows chickens a mule the food
they ate the way they talked my dad's music
my mother's reading books aloud to us boys
the Wytheville radio station daffodils lilacs
cigarette smoke the weather bumble bees
my grandparents' fighting at Sunday dinner
my parents' deep care for us and each other.

What Can You Tell Me About Your Father?

Around people he was rarely at ease
but when he could settle into himself—
reading the *Roanoke Times,* watching TV,
or paying bills—he seemed comfortable.
I studied him when we had company.
He had nice manners, asked polite questions,
tried not to talk about himself—I think he
feared being the center of attention.
What he liked best was when mother's Uncle
Bo came to our house to play chess with him.
Reticent as a tree and deeply humble,
that man and my father played their slow games
saying almost nothing. Did they have fun?
I can't say. But those games went on and on.

What About Your Mother?

Tempestuous, meaning *temperamental,*
hot-blooded, mercurial—long before
we knew the words we knew the individual
who embodied them. Of course we adored
her but we also feared her. Little boys,
my brothers and I couldn't know how young
she was or that before we were born she'd lost
a girl baby. A beautiful woman
in her mid-twenties in a big old house
at the end of a dirt road with the three
of us & no nanny to help—miraculous
she didn't just drive away to the city.
She spanked us with a hairbrush when she got mad,
but she was our mother—that's what mothers did.

Art for Money

It's a sad fact about our culture that a poet can earn much
more money writing or talking about his art than he can
by practicing it.
    —W. H. AUDEN

A little boy, I'd pick dandelion bouquets
for my mother, who would then do her best
to feign delight over the droopy clump
of weeds I'd shyly handed her.
                                This lasted
a week or two. Then I caught on to her fake
joy, she grew tired of the game, so we stopped
and that was that.
                    I've been paid for poems—
it felt like money I'd found in the grass.
Truth is I like a regular paycheck
for work I've done in a classroom. Talking,
yes, but work nevertheless.
                            What's stayed
with me?
            How my mother's blue eyes flashed that first
time I lifted posies to her in my sweaty fist.

What Are You Up To?

What five syllables are more common more
friendly don't they insinuate an almost
familial affection between speaker
and spoken-to my father posed this question
if he came upon me reading of course
he meant to suggest I was a rascally
kind of boy and he loved me anyway
but he could see I was up to nothing
if anything I was down to zero
identity was entirely eyeballs
story and words innocent of even
the childish crimes I had in fact committed
but I liked it that he asked me that
question winking at me as he walked away.

Elrica

My grandmother's sister, dead half a century
now, is the only person I've known
to have that name. Loud, obese, unschooled,
and opinionated, she was always

the center of attention. Uncle Jack Kent,
her husband, whom she treated like a servant,
did the cooking and housecleaning, fixed her drinks,
helped her bathe and dress, was as sweet-tempered

a man as I've ever known. From age eight
to twelve, I found them disturbing, but I hung
around, studying them when I should have
gone outside to play. I think of them often—

those two perfectly content to be unhappy.
I can't name whatever it was they taught me.

Some Kitchens

The average American family kitchen contains more
then ten thousand food or food-related items.
— *Culinary Miscellany,* VOLUME VI

Forever held in mind are my mother's
and Grandmama Huddle's in Ivanhoe;
Gran and Aunt Stella's in Newbern; the ones
Lindsey and I had in Roanoke, New York,

and Essex Center; Joe and Teresa's
in Winchester; Molly and Ray's in Winooski;
Bess and Nick's in Oregon (Wisconsin)—
I could, if ordered to do so or face

a firing squad, write my life history
in terms of kitchens I've known—where mother
kept the baking soda, the scent of fried
chicken Thelma made for Sunday dinner, Aunt

Murrell's iced tea. These particulars matter
only to me, to whom they're like scripture.

Girl with Bare Arms

> The girls on the street are a joy. A girl with bare
> arms by the St. Regis; a girl with bare shoulders on
> Fifty-seventh Street; dark eyes and light eyes and red
> hair and above all the wonderful sense of dignity
> and purpose in their clear features.
> —JOHN CHEEVER

Mr. Cheever was a naughty saint who found
the world and its human inhabitants
simultaneously desirable
and holy. He couldn't stop himself from looking.
Our witty American Chekhov (not
to say he didn't suffer), his nature
was both divine and bawdy; therefore he
he had to use his wit to defend himself
from despair and the urge to kill himself.
As for that girl by the St. Regis—yes,
she felt his eyes violate and praise her
but found it possible not to hate him,
mostly because he kept walking. God bless
him, I say, as he goes on blessing us.

How Do You Pray?

Since I grew up in a church I still have
the praying inclination though I've come
to think of God—which is to say science
and coincidence—as neither inclined nor
capable of listening but my prayer habit
kicks in anyway and so I'll hear a voice
from that churchy part of my brain begin
O Lord please— followed by a request to
turn fate this way or that, but I rarely
get very far with the ask because when I
put it into words shame comes down on me
I become aware of the millions of people
suffering unspeakable hardship pain loss
Lord I'll shut up now. Ignore me please.

The Lonesome Animal

And God stepped out on space,
And he looked around and said:
I'm lonely—
I'll make me a world.
—James Weldon Johnson

We are lonesome animals. We spend all life trying to be less
lonesome.
—John Steinbeck

. . . I in my north room dance naked, grotesquely before my
mirror waving my shirt round my head and singing softly to
myself: "I am lonely, lonely. I was born to be lonely, I am best so!"
—William Carlos Williams

So it comes down to us from this God who
got shazzamed into the universe and who
lost interest in playing with lightning
bolts and designing giraffes and beetles—

this God who sounded out *lone-ly* to describe
the hitch in his pulse, his hunger for food
he'd never tasted, his restless eyes scanning
paradise and finding it somehow lacking—

this God whose feet kept tripping him up
with dance moves, this god who wanted to touch
something that would touch back, this God who wept
when wolves and coyotes answered him with sounds

that shivered his bones. And then this God got it!
Lone-ly meant *alive. Lone-ly* was *divine.*

Is Nothing Sacred?

The bunny that dashed across our street just
before dawn this morning—a fast-moving
rabbit shadow that crackled with holiness
for two blinks of my eyes. In Bruce Springsteen's
"Growin' Up," there's a drum solo that makes
me weepy with joy, and in Duke Ellington's
"Take the A Train," when the brass section kicks
in, that energy rattles my skeleton,
and when I visit *Girl with a Red Hat,*
time stops for me so that other viewers
have to navigate around the pillar of salt
I've become. My problem is the reverse
of yours—there's no shortage of sacred,
it's everywhere. I try not to be scared.

Take a Look at This

Skittish geniuses of staying out
of sight, warblers are the ones we most want
to see—or photograph, as is the case
with me, because I consider what I've seen

to be perishable, whereas this picture
is not only permanent testimony
to what my eyes took in and a somewhat
artful composition, it's an act I

committed in response to a creature
whose seven grams of life is beyond
miraculous, an act that required cunning
and effort—each of us struggling against

what the other wanted, warbler and I
colluding to make this heartbeat of light.

How to Enter a Cosmic Quirk

for Amy Appel

You need a car with a pretty good sound system. You need
"Growin' Up" Track #7 of Disc 1 of Springsteen & the E
Street Band—Live/1975–85, and you need to be driving on
a highway where there's not a lot of traffic. Time of day or
night doesn't much matter, but ideally you'll be up on the Blue
Ridge Parkway mid-morning with a little coffee buzz going
for you. When the tune starts up, listen at any volume—Bruce's
words tumble out and the band's beat generates that antsy
energy of a kid about fifteen who's smart and mouthy and
recently wise to the stupendously deep bullshit of the adult
world. The spirit here is Dylan Thomas updated, Americanized,
& surly with a guitar & drum set installed in his brain. But
right now you don't have to try to listen carefully, you'll hear
all you need to with only one ear. The first couple of verses
will slide right on through your skull, then there'll come this
electric pinging, one note, maybe an E-flat an octave and a half
above middle C. This is where Bruce starts up his monologue,
and it's pretty good the first fifty or sixty times you hear it, very
New Jersey and funny and it'll win your heart for the kid that
Springsteen must have been, precocious musician probably
from about age twelve and therefore at odds with his family
in general and his dad in particular. Here you need to turn
the volume up a couple notches just to keep track of where
Bruce is in the narrative, because he's taking his time, building
up to what really matters. When he gets to the part where his
dad is bugging him about his career choices and his mom is
advising him that he oughta be a lawyer or an author because
that way he'll get a little something for himself, why then you
need your fingers on that volume control, the moment is very
close and you'll want to time it precisely. Bruce's voice will lift,

he'll almost shout, *Well, tonight they're just gonna have to settle for ROCK & ROLL!* Right THERE you want that volume maxed up as high as you can stand it without deafing yourself, because what happens now is every drum kit and electric guitar all up and down the Jersey Shore has suddenly joined in and simultaneously begun generating the most prison-breaking, lobotomizing musical thunder a human being will ever experience—it's this gorgeous rolling wave of noise that contains your birth, your childhood, peace, war, blues, jazz, the deaths of your grandparents, and the future of your unborn children. That sound will resonate through your whole body, it will carry you out to sea to play with the dolphins in the bright sunlight, and then when Bruce picks up the words again, you can gradually turn the volume down, because you're being carried back home in the arms of your dad who will kiss your forehead and put you to bed. That's when you need to check out your speedometer, because you'll be speeding alright, and if you don't get that vehicle slowed down pretty quick, you're going to fly right off the highway and meet a tree or a rock or maybe run your car right through the middle of somebody's living room. Trouble is, you won't mind a bit—you'll already have flown with the angels who have loved you.

Before the Concert

The thing worthwhile is always unplanned. Any art that
is a result of preconcerted plans is a dead baby.
    —WILLA CATHER

That smush of chatter, orchestral cacophony,
dimming lights, perfume, and cologne tickles
the mind, riles the blood, calls forth the divine
pranksters.
            The way the word *décolletage*
shimmers as lexical pornography
all through the auditorium with the girls
and ladies having harnessed their bosoms
so as both to hide and display
                        that beauty
inviting all creation to sing and dance.
We'll get Rachmaninoff or Tchaikovsky
on our way to the Crossroads or the Canal
Street Brothel.
            We don't quite know what we want,
but we recognize it when we hear it—*song*
the lightning bolt jolting us back to life.

What Would You Like?

The *Would* makes the question interesting.
It casts doubt on whether you have something
I want and whether you're willing to bring
it to me. Also, you could be suggesting
that I am psycho-spiritually
incapable of articulating
my deepest yearning. Pie with ice cream?
To be at peace with God? Stimulating
and comfortable lives for my children?
All that, yes, and more, but I can't seem
to imagine or name the one sublime thing.
I don't even see its shadow in my brain.
Hate to be a pain and sorry to trouble you,
but I guess I need more time with the menu.

Is That It?

Verb and two antecedentless pronouns
is hardly a promising beginning:
If "That" refers to somebody's last ounce
of whiskey or dope or information
then we have to address the black hole of "It,"
which could mean a falling leaf, the history
of civilization, my relationship
with you, or the tantalizing mystery
of why the African spurred tortoise
walks with his human through Tsukishima.
I admit I watch animal videos,
but this poem is serious. It may not seem a
mindful composition but believe me,
that turtle is something you need to see!

My Surly Heart

[A great singer needs] a big chest,
a big mouth, 90 percent memory,
10 percent intelligence, lots of hard
work, and something in the heart.
—ENRICO CARUSO

The aim of literature . . . is the
creation of a strange object covered
with fur which breaks your heart.
—DONALD BARTHELME

You don't know what lives
in there until you ask it
to help you make some art

*Fall in love with someone
run a marathon befriend a
homeless person I'll help*

*you with those things art
is too hard plus it makes
me feel strange* it whines

*Look what it did to Plath
Berryman Jimi Hendrix Van
Gogh Kurt Cobain Basquiat*

Rothko and Billie Holiday
Heart I beg you I want to
sing arias paint gorgeous

visions write novels that
will inspire people to be
kind to each other I want—

Don't be an idiot I'm not
that kind of heart you're
not ready to make the art

I could help you with you
can be an okay accountant
look at your tidy columns

the kind of art you'd get
with my help will horrify
your mother make your dad

angry turn your potential
girlfriends cold keep you
poor forever trust me art

I help you with will make
you feel dissatisfied all
day teach you how failure

disfigures the soul turns
you permanently eccentric
disqualifies you—
                    Enough!

How about we say no songs
no paintings no novels or
memoirs just a poem every

now and then? Heart turns
in my chest lurches skips
syncopates finally growls

Hate the stuff can't help
you—
　　　　Yes you can you know
you can just one poem you

can do that for me to get
me started—
　　　　Gonna be mean
as a mistreated porcupine—

I don't care, I just want
to feel like a poet Heart
snarls *OK pal you got it.*

What Can I Say?

Perhaps you've already said too much so you
have an opportunity here to pause
and let silence have its say. To eschew
mindless syllables is to bless
the conversation with an opening
for those fresh and intelligent words for which
we've long yearned. The ratio of inane
to scintillating shows that idiots
dominate our discourse, so that keeping
quiet can actually improve the IQ
of social intercourse. Try to listen
more than you talk. Think of the good you'll do.
I reserve the right to remain silent.
If anybody asks, you can say that.

Composition as Ethical Inquiry

A man who has faith, intelligence, and cultivation will show that
in his work.
　　—WALKER EVANS

I hate to advocate drugs, alcohol, violence, or insanity to anyone,
but they've always worked for me.
　　—HUNTER S. THOMPSON

The welcome universe, the rain that sounded through the world of
apples had vanished. Filth was his destiny, his best self, and he began
with relish a long ballad called The Fart that Saved Athens.
　　—JOHN CHEEVER, "THE WORLD OF APPLES"

When this cultivated man sits down to explicate
a particularly exquisite Henry James paragraph,
after hours of stillness, he understands he prefers
silence to the tepid brilliance of James's prose.

A man who loathes himself sits down to chronicle his
fistfights, his betrayals of friends, family, and many
a good woman—then finds himself humming Amazing Grace
and writing prayers for prisoners on death row in America.

In her writing classes, Deborah Eisenberg says again
and again, "The sentence, the sentence, the sentence."
Impartial, merciless, it will have its way with you.
In the chamber of diction and syntax the truth of you

shall be revealed: artist, monk, assassin, penitent,
athlete, nurse, dancer, perfect fool of a president.

What?!

This brazen little all-purpose spitball
of a syllable just interrobangs
its way into silences of unusual
perplexity or comic sturm and drang.
It's especially apt for ancient
family donnybrooks like when you said I snatched
your sippy cup out of your hands, a blatant
lie that shuts up everyone but Uncle Mitch
who's amused by our chronic goofiness
and goes giggly over his mashed potatoes
so we give him the death stare, he glances
all around the table, makes google eyes,
then just shouts it in that quexclamation
tone that makes us all guffaw about nothing.

The Braid

Like a black flame it hugs her spine.
Or like an eel. Or like a sword.
I'd kill with it if it were mine.
  —Barbara Greenberg, "The Braid"

A girl walked in. In stories this is where
I lean forward. Just so, she held her head,
her braid woven strand over strand, her hair

almost lacquered it was fixed with such care
and catching the light. Did you see, you said,
that girl who walked in? The story of her

braid would take a while to tell. Did I stare
at her? Everyone at our table did.
The precisely woven strands of her hair

in that braid *took dominion everywhere,*
yes, and a *slovenly wilderness* we'd
been until she walked in. This story's her

property, you know, and you and I are,
too, in this telling of it. If her braid
was woven from those tiny strands of our

attention, then we were objects, we were
little dolls fixed to see her, little dead
parts of her story. She walked into where
we waited for her braid, her life, her hair.

How Does This Look?

It is the stunning truth of you, my dear!
Such panache to wear a floor-length codpiece
and I'm dazzled by your Saran wrap brassiere!
Those cow-patty sandals with soccer cleats—
they make my heart jitterbug in my chest!
Connoisseurs of haute couture will worship
at your feet for decades; they will say this
ensemble redefined the basic concept
of wearing clothes from Cro-Magnon culture
through Lady Gaga. That pubic-hair purse
is forcefully eloquent, and those vulture-
talon epaulettes are both blessing and curse.
Now darling tell your date, after the prom
your parents say you must come straight home.

Do You Live Here?

well yes I'm breathing I'm here so I must
live here helpless and blind we have to fight
our way out of darkness and turns out that's
our destination a round-trip ticket
instead of dust to dust it's nothingness
to nothingness but we do get this whatever
you call it flash of lilacs sex giraffes
springtime wine love music just not forever
but yes my wife and I own a house up
the hill a few blocks we've raised our children
here we like to say this is home for us
good schools nice restaurants shall we go in
to this place and raise a glass to being mortal
great food in here nice kids waiting tables.

Curmudgeon's Song

From a distance I hear something soft, sung
as though someone knew half the words, was shy.
I want a song this spring against hate. The young

go out to loll in the grass, their coats flung
aside, forgotten as winter, and I
go walking toward what's so softly sung.

I almost lose it. I hurry among
crowds of laughers, dazed gazers at the sky.
This spring I want a song against hate. The young

get in my way, their bright colored packs slung
across their backs, careless of passersby,
while far ahead I can barely hear it, sung

so sweetly words shape themselves on my tongue.
Wait! I know that song. I can tell you why
in spring you sing against hate. Oh, the young

don't know this. Did I tell you that I've rung
bells in May, that I've known I wouldn't die?
But why this distance, this thing softly sung
so far away? In spring I hate the young.

How Old Are You?

My body says I'm seventy six my face
says no no I'm approaching a hundred
my brain's ad hoc whatever polymorphous
lunchtime maybe forty bedtime half-dead
sometimes in exuberant dreams it says
it's my birthday party I'm six years old
opening presents foolish with happiness
or I'm thirteen and just about to go
downstairs with Melva to play whistle stop
in her basement but why quantify it
in years why not days right now I'm up
to twenty-six thousand three hundred and eight
if I'm the prisoner of my life then that's
my number I mean why not be precise?

Drinking Alone by Moonlight

—after Li Bai's "Drinking Alone By Moonlight"

The moon damns a man drinking wine alone—
he'd wanted to bloom in the silver light
but the intimacy he found was with himself,
the cup he lifted purest solitude. So many

people hovering in the shadows—he couldn't
understand the sounds he heard. *My body
is out here, too!* he shouted. Into the silence
that followed he whispered, *Is this temporary?*

Wine cheers a fellow, he thought. It'll be
spring soon. Ah, but the damning moon shone
ruthlessly across his arms and shoulders.
The man shuffled his feet, told them to dance,

but no one emerged from the shadows to become
his friend. The man imagined himself as cinders
scattered over dirt and pavement, ashes sifted into
water. Then the man understood the moon was about

to disperse him out into the great river of stars.
He'd have to sober up, have to stop whining. But oh,
the place he was going would be his companion—he'd be
the cloud, she the sunlight blazing him up gold.

Are You Happy?

In the smiley-face sense of the word—yes,
I get bursts of goofy energy that
lift me sky high but then drop me so fast
I feel foolish. I prefer those slow pleasant
stretches of time when I'm doing something
I enjoy—reading, watching birds, mowing the grass—
paying no attention to my feelings.
Unaware of myself is when I'm happiest.
A friend of mine said his dad's last words were,
"Dan, I really liked to eat," but I wolf
my food, greedily stuffing more and more
gastric pleasure down my gullet. If
I had my way there'd be no word for it.
One look and you'd know if I was or wasn't.

The Househusband Speaks His Piece

A *househusband* is a male person living with his partner
and performing all the housework and duties that have
traditionally been associated with a housewife.
—URBAN DICTIONARY

I took on these duties in a high pout
some forty years ago, and this morning
unloading the dishwasher while I fixed
our coffee I grappled with the epiphany

that I was born to put away salad bowls,
glasses, dishes, and flatware; to make
beds, do laundry, and tidy up the house
when company's coming; to plan and cook

our meals, clean up and put the kitchen
in order, grocery shop at five different
stores, buy ant traps and paper products,
clean the refrigerator—and these details

that make you yawn are of such deep interest
to me that I savor them like hidden sweets.

Idiosyncrasy

Vast collection like I try to
make my bed while I'm still in it
can't leave the house or lock
   the car w/o patting the keys
    in my pocket have to walk through
     the graveyard twice a day or else
      feel half-wonky yes I converse
       with those folks up there what's
       wrong with that? I say hi sweetie
to chickadees hey baby to cardinals
& oh man to the big blue heron yes
well I also give advice to myself
 while walking & don't anymore even
  think about saying it aloud if
    my flatware isn't fixed the way
     mother taught me I fix it myself
     like she'd whispered in my ear
    I rotate shampoos feel obligated
to wash between my toes walk
through the dark house while drying
off after my shower shave twice once
in each direction oh I know this is
tiresome I wouldn't want to know all
this about you but I haven't even
 gotten started & here's what's
   scary my collection is growing a baby
    I had none whatsoever was so normal
     nurses wanted to steal me an old man
     now I've got so many I could pay off
    the national debt if they were worth
a dollar apiece hey & some are
downright priceless like my inclination

to eat pie or pizza from the back
corner toward the front the way I take
my vitamins biggest to smallest
the way I try to sing tenor harmony
 with the groaning noise my coffee
  maker makes the way I suspect it
   might be the only thing in my life
    that completely accepts me loves me
     for what I am & gives me what I want.

Are You Sure?

When I am I think I probably ought
not to be when I say I am & then
it turns out I'm wrong the embarrassment
can be instructive depending on how open
to character-building I am my wife keeps
informal statistics on which one of us
is right in our little disagreements
she's far ahead & her numbers serve as
a humbling force in my household conduct
& attitude I am insufferably
uncertain & free to be as corrupt
as I want in what I say. Think of me
as an unrepentantly loose cannon
Mayor of the Town of Usually Wrong.

Bliss Happens

I have this theory about dialogue
and compatibility—you know how
in *For Esmé with Love and Squalor* you
want the scene in the tea room with the boy,
the charmingly precocious Esmé,
and the soldier narrator to go on
and on, because their talk—the melody,
cadence and tone, the boy's interruptions—
it's talk that charms the heart. I've had it in real
life—folks who conversed with me the way Armstrong
and Fitzgerald sang duets. Sex appeal
had nothing to do with a conversation
I once had with a cashier at Price Chopper,
a small-talk aria that came close to rapture.

How Bad Is It?

Well it's worse now than when it was really
bad but when it was really bad we all said
this is just a few little rocks in the chili
you should have seen it when the moon pretended
it was tired of us and didn't show itself
from April through August romance went south
nobody got pregnant sex lives came to a halt
we impeached the president even though
she was a nice lady who said it was
Republicans who stole the moon and watch out
they'd take the sun too if they could but the worst
was yet to come which is always the way of it
sure it's bad but I feel more like I do
now than I did a while ago don't you?

What Is Wrong With Me?

Not so many things well let's say maybe
a dozen or so my craving to be
admired my erratic ways of loving
my rush to judge people negatively
my quick temper and my incoherence
when I'm angry I sputter and curse when
I'm capable of calm clear argument
lack of curiosity impatience
vanity forgetfulness carelessness
fits of generosity followed by
frugality that's random & pointless
irregular hygiene sometimes my fly
doesn't get zipped same can be said about
my mouth it's open when it should be shut.

How Many Times Do I Have to Tell You?

Arithmetic's obviously not what's
at issue here, and interrogative
though your sentence is, you and I know it's
not a real question, it's just some abusive
noise you need to make. What you want is
for me to bow my head, say I'm sorry,
and more or less acknowledge your genius
and my stupidity. Our history
is boss to worker, teacher to student,
parent to child, with you always being
the MFWIC—the Motherfucker What's in
Charge. It's how we like it, don't you think?
You know what I'm going to do—not even
blink and say like I'm half-listening, "Seven."

What's Real?

This question didn't much interest me
until after my hearing and eyesight
got so bad that what had been merely
something the excessively erudite
discussed when they were bored became a test
of my sanity. Then the gunshots from
up the street turned out to be a truck's
backfiring, the open pit at the bottom
of a staircase became a shadow I could
actually step on without falling into hell,
and the end table where I set my cold
glass of beer never existed at all.
Old age tells you if you're an idiot
or a saint. Either way you won't like it.

Where's Your Faith?

I believe in art that takes us beyond
ourselves gives us all it's got but remains
indifferent if we don't understand
or like or care about it art explains
us to ourselves by way of our senses
lets us live all of human history
births us kills us then brings us back to life
again says pray though nothing's listening
lingers in our minds lives in our dreams
tells us not to fear winter it always
yields to spring and the dark only seems
a threat it thinks we're okay softly says
try to get some sleep now don't worry
just close your eyes I'll tell you a story.

Finch Dream

Baby-fist-sized darts of gold streak the air
around feeder and bath, they weave in low
around porch posts, swerve past house, tree, and car.

Local angels, these spring-crazed finches are
hot for each other, sun-drops of yellow
we miss if we blink, gold looping the air.

Rocketing our planet toward hell, we're
disconsolate, staring out our windows
at blurred birds zipping past house, tree, and car—

their flighty exuberance stops us where
we stand. Small brains, tiny hearts, do they know
how we oafs feel when their gold fires the air?

Once I walked through high grass where hundreds were
feeding and they flew up before me, they rose
like a dream—no houses or cars, just birds

rising in swooping arcs, splotches of fire
invented by the sky and the spring meadow.
I walked among gold flashes streaking the air.
Houses and cars all gone. Finches everywhere.

What Do You Like to Eat?

Do we have to use that word it always
makes me think of our bodies as pipelines
where we stuff food to convert it to waste
creatures of the planet throughout time
a huge system designed to produce piss
and shit oh god it's disgusting give me
dine consume nibble or even *gobble* please
can't we just take a step back and try to see
the great current flowing though our human
insides made up of animals and plants
even the air and the sea think how wind
enters a forest without a sound I still can't
stand somebody chewing loudly it makes me sick
but yes I'm kind of bonkers holistic.

How Do You Feel About Your Body?

Duck-footed it's got toenail fungus asthma
a gut bad eyesight lousy hearing achy joints
but if I were trying to sell it I'd say
damn good body that needs daily maintenance
a nap toast a banana for breakfast
a light lunch salad and meat for dinner
a couple of beers some fruit it's spent
just one night in a hospital in all these years
it's got dermatology issues cancer's
got the hots for it body sings in the car
though its chops are shot it's no dancer
but will dance with or without a partner
fears suffering thinks it's got enough courage
to face death but hates the hell out of old age.

Dumetella Carolinensis

I can stare at Catbird taking a two-minute
bath in the black dish beside my garden fountain,
then stare another minute or two while it shakes,
fluffs and preens its feathers.
                              Lord God
of the Galaxy, I know You've been amused
by the joke of hell for sinners and the reward
of heaven for the pious among us.
                              I suspect You
of listening to our prayers as we watch sitcoms,
the news, and sports.
                    How can they be such fools?
I see You shaking Your divine head over our
everlasting buffoonery.
                              Meanwhile Catbird has
this twitch and point thing it does with its tail—
a purely exuberant gesture that can be expressed
only by a creature that flies.
                              Galactic Lord God,
Catbird denies You painted its backside the bright
orange of a Texas Longhorn football jersey, denies
it wears Your black thumbprint on its skull,
                                        Catbird
twitches and points that jaunty tail, wings off up
into the cedar tree where I can barely see it,
unleashes an aria that roughly translates to
                                        *This
is your allotment of joy for the next two weeks
Speak to me no more of this Lord God of the Galaxy
you have invented, I am Catbird, Inventor and Boss
of myself,*
            and so should you wish to express gratitude

44

for some slight sliver of joy in your dismal gravity-
bound death-fearing nights and days, from now on
address your remarks to Me, Catbird, Sublime Singer
and Bather. I may or may not get back to you.

Would You Repeat the Question Please?

for Jane Ambrose

Pew after pew of us gray-haired mourners
our smiles those of living ghosts acting like
Jane's dead but she's here somewhere of course
we can't see her but she's sort of alive. . . .
From way back death's been our moody girlfriend
scrunched up against the passenger-side door
won't talk won't smile just smokes & pouts she'd end
the relationship if we'd just stop the car
but lately she's gotten friendlier this
past year she put her hand on my thigh her tongue
in my ear O Jane why did you say yes
to that cunning bitch remember how once
we were children sitting at desks in school
with you our droll girl liveliest of us all?

Villanelle for Lady Day

She was arrested for narcotics possession in 1947 and made
to serve time in jail. After her release, she sold out a show at
Carnegie Hall. Still, she could not make a clean break from
heroin and the police forces trying to punish her for it. As
she lay dying in her hospital bed from liver cirrhosis in 1959,
she was handcuffed and arrested for drug possession.
—*The Writer's Almanac*, APRIL 7, 2017

Hateful America, I wore your uniform
five years after Lady Day died in handcuffs—
Genteel racist, I was born to conform.

Discharged in '66 I wore my airborne
cap home, saluted my grandfather as if
he should have been proud of me in that uniform.

Billie said, "If I'm going to sing like someone
else, then I don't need to sing at all." Let's
just say I was white and knew how to conform.

I didn't hear "Strange Fruit" until she'd been
long dead. By then even Ali'd gotten his
notice and had to wear that hateful uniform.

He said, "I ain't got no quarrel with them
Viet Cong," but they took him anyway, and Elvis,
too—they made them stand up straight and conform

just enough to stay out of jail. My shame
is some of who I am—I've got my campaign
badge, my honorable discharge—but just minutes
ago I learned her real name was Eleanora Fagan.

47

O Say Can You See?

The national anthem starts making you
an American crazy before you're born
thirty thousand six hundred & forty-two
times I figure I've heard it I was in
my high school band I watch a lot of sports
I know all the words when somebody sings
it on TV I hum the tenor part
when I'm in hell it'll be the last thing
that gets burned away from me I've renounced
my hometown I've disavowed the south
& I've lately come to see how my country
'tis a nightmare no more pledge of allegiance
for me I can't help it I'm American
can't get this God damn song out of my brain.

Proof that An Old-Testament God Exists

The one we chose to lead us made it clear
hating was his best talent, his second
best was bullying, he could love only
himself, his measure of others was how

much money they had and what they could
do for him, he respected only dictators,
was most comfortable around con men
and thugs, and considered women objects

to be fondled or else ignored. It was
as if King Herod had run for president,
campaigned on his nastiness of character
and the Murder of the Innocents. This week

he took children away from their parents
and locked them up. Guess what comes next.

Animal Videos as Last-Resort Religious Practice of the Ruined Nation

When politics became so deceitful
and hateful that even the idiot
president himself could see the country
collapsing into chaos, we citizens

found the old comforts—food, music, booze, drugs,
sex, and our churches—helped only a little
and though suicide rates shot up, most of us
lacked the nerve and/or the means to blow out

our own candles, so we turned to the videos—
an owl befriending an orphaned llama,
a baby elephant chasing geese, the Japanese man
taking his giant tortoise for a walk. We knew

they weren't going to save us, but they were
all we could find that made us feel better.

What Time Is It?

Time of the young white man shooting nine black
people in a South Carolina church; of ISIS
flourishing in Syria and Iraq,
beheading hostages, killing whole families.
Time of white police shooting young unarmed
black men; of kidnapping and enslaving
girls in Africa; of the Arab Spring turned
into chaos; of countries self-destructing.
Time of glaciers melting, California
drying up, tornadoes, flash floods, oil spills;
of ignorance, megalomania,
and greed; of the world in an evil spell.
Last night I held my two-year-old grandchild.
She asked me to put her down, and I did.

Two and a Half

> . . . the son with his
> right hand on the handrail,
> the father, left hand on the left,
> and in the middle they were
> holding hands, and when I neared,
> they opened the simple gate
> of their interwoven fingers
> to let me pass, then reached out
> for each other and continued on.
> —TED KOOSER, "TWO"

At family dinner last
Sunday evening we held
hands for the grace, seven
of us around the table,
Phoebe who's two and a half
taking my left hand (my right
holding her Aunt Bess's), Phoebe
the granddaughter who loves
the whole family to sing
Happy Birthday to Baby Jesus,
whom she'd plucked from his crib
in the crèche to carry with her
all through the house, this Phoebe
twelve words into the blessing
jerked her hand from mine and looked
at me as if I'd tried
to steal her Baby Jesus
and wouldn't ever give it back.

Trees R Not Us

It's safe to assume trees don't think, at least
not the way humans, ants, flies, or turtles do,
but their lives are subtle and complex, it's just

that they don't make choices. Weather, birds, insects,
machines, governments—and most certainly you
and I—determine a tree's fate. The lowest

creature—a wooly worm, say—an almost brainless
form of life but a thing that moves from here to
there, turns toward the sun sinking in the west

and slightly shifts some moisture, which act affects
plus or minus the lifespan of an ancient spruce.
So it's really better that trees don't have thoughts,

because then they'd have dreams—of the loveliest
day in a thousand years, light rain, sun, a cool
breeze, two scarlet tanagers that stayed long past

dark. And if dreams then nightmares—of pink-faced
developers, bulldozers, truckloads of tools.
It's safe to assume if trees had bad dreams, the worst
would be men hauling chainsaws into the forest.

What's the Best Death You Can Imagine?

In my sleep of course or at least at home
& maybe with Lindsey & Bess & Molly
close by so I can say goodbye and tell them
how much I love them and that I'm sorry
I didn't do better by them. I don't
want to die in a hospital unless
there's no other way. I'd prefer not
to be in pain, I want it to happen fast,
& then I want everybody who's cared
about me to know I had more than enough
life, a ton of good times, way more than my share
of love, & few regrets. Forgive this truth—
I've never really dreaded death. In the art
we love endings are always the best part.

Desirable Madness

It is a delicious thing to write, to be no longer
yourself but to move in an entire universe of your
own creating. Today, for instance, as man and
woman, both lover and mistress, I rode in a forest on
an autumn afternoon under the yellow leaves, and I
was also the horses, the leaves, the wind, the words
my people uttered, even the red sun that made
them almost close their love-drowned eyes.
    —GUSTAVE FLAUBERT

Ray Bradbury never liked to know what he was
doing or where he was going when he wrote—
he just hammered out the words from "the secret
motives within." It took him ten days to write
Fahrenheit 451. Ten days to run up-and-down stairs
and pull books off shelves to find random quotes
for his book. Ten days not knowing what he was
writing, just following the course of the words
that tumbled out of his head to tell their tale.
    —*The Writer's Almanac*

I am not an eccentric. It's just that I am more alive
than most people. I am an unpopular electric eel
in a pool of catfish.
    —EDITH SITWELL

Some commit murder, some must take drugs
their whole lives, some must go to prison
or the asylum, but some certain ones receive
fellowships, grants, money from patrons,
endowed chairs, or just ongoing support
from understanding partners or spouses.

Our culture sorts all of us out, doesn't it?
Of course we are our culture, and sometimes
—e.g. the US in 2017, or cities and towns
where ISIS enforces its laws—the culture itself
is crazier than any individual could ever be.

My family sent my Aunt Inez to the asylum
in Marion after she pushed my brother off
the back porch one afternoon after Sunday
family dinner. They sent her home after some
years of receiving electroshock therapy.
She lived with Grandma Lawson until that
old woman died, then she lived by herself
in a dusty old house in the middle of town.

Dead maybe sixty years, Inez comes alive
in my thoughts occasionally though she
and I never talked—she spoke only to her
mother, my father, and the people we hired
to take her food and do some cleaning.
Inez cut her own hair, wore worn-out men's
jeans and a t-shirt, scared away children
who'd come to stare through her windows.
It's too bad Alfred Hitchcock never saw her;
he'd have put her in a movie where she could
have played the part of a little town's crazy
woman, supported by a family that wanted
nothing to do with her. In the falling-down
garage beside the house there was an ancient
Ford she'd driven as a teenage girl; inside
the house, in bureau drawers in her bedroom,
we found a collection of used menstrual pads

and band aids, and not much more—except four
astrological charts so elaborately drawn they
were works of what we'd now call "outsider
art"—one for herself and one for each
of her sisters—Ida, Elrica, and Dunkley.

I'm writing these words a thousand miles
north of that town in a house that's a palace
compared to the one in which Inez Lawson
lived out her final years. I think I must
be doing it to try to correct an injustice
that resists any correcting. I know I should
put my effort into helping my country heal.
Here in Burlington, at busy intersections
where cars must stop, there stand homeless
men and women holding handmade signs asking
for help. In Madison, Wisconsin, last month,
a block away from the state capital building,
in the 7 a.m. cold, walking from my hotel
to Starbucks, I stepped past a blue tarpaulin
covering an invisible human being sleeping
in a doorway, someone living like a dead
person in a culture that's siphoning wealth
upward from citizens who desperately need it
into the banking accounts of citizens who
live so extravagantly they'd think this is
a comedy I'm writing—a story about a madwoman
painstakingly creating charts of the stars that
aligned to give her and her sisters the lives
they had. And the lives they didn't have.

Distraction and Composition

I don't think Hank done it this way.
—WAYLON JENNINGS

The spring garden and the birds that visit
are my companions for the early hours
when I try to write. I look up and away
often and keep my camera handy in case

a warbler, thrush, or wren presents itself.
Squirrels and chipmunks raid the bird
feeders, and a sly raven glides in to
rinse his scavenged pizza slices, French fries,

or sandwich scraps in the bird bath. I shout
at the raven and use the garden hose
to squirt the rodents. Thus the world
calls me to take a break every few minutes.

Tolstoy and Shakespeare would disapprove,
but where are they now? I'm the one who's alive.

Mood Indigo

Ellington voices the trombone right at the top of the
instrument's register, and the clarinet at the very lowest.
—WIKIPEDIA

This morning's end-of-April shower grants
me a glimpse of a goldfinch on the bare limb
of my neighbor's birch tree. The grey-blue sky
releases raindrops that puddle on the stones

just beyond my French doors, helping the grass
go greener by the minute. Ellington's
composition might have begun sounding
its meditative joy in his mind's ear

on a morning just like this. Others may
call this a gloomy day, but my seventy-six
years have taught me to recognize what I need
when I see it coming—my death dancing alone

in its blue gown. I know just what to say:
"Oh, there you are, my dear, may I join you?"

ACKNOWLEDGMENTS

"What Are You Up To?," "What Can I Say?," and "How Do You Feel About Your Body?" appeared in *Green Mountains Review,* 29/1 (2016); "What Can You Tell Me About Your Father?" and "Would You Repeat the Question Please?" appear in *Roads Taken: Contemporary Vermont Poetry* (Green Writers Press, 2017); "What's Real" and "Is Nothing Sacred" appeared in *Plume #64;* and "*Dumetella Carolinensis*" appeared in *Plume Anthology #6.*

The following poems have appeared in *Verse Virtual:* "Is That It" (July 17); "How to Enter a Cosmic Quirk" (January 2017); "Where Do You Come From" and "Where's Your Faith" (December 2016); "O Say Can You See" (November 2016); "Finch Dream" (July 2016). www.verse-virtual.com/

"Animal Videos as Last-Resort Religious Practice of the Ruined Nation," "Proof That an Old Testament God Exists," and "Composition as Ethical Inquiry" appeared in https://voxpopulisphere.com/

In a slightly different version, "Desirable Madness" appeared in *On the Seawall: A Community Gathering for New Writing and Commentary:* www.facebook.com/ontheseawall/

CPSIA information can be obtained
at www.ICGtesting.com
Printed in the USA
LVHW112145081019
633637LV00001B/327/P